An I Can Read Book®

Danny and the Dinosaur

Story and Pictures by SYD HOFF

HarperCollinsPublishers

This book is a presentation of Newfield Publications, Inc.
Newfield Publications offers book clubs for children
from preschool through high school. For further
information write to: **Newfield Publications, Inc.,**
4343 Equity Drive, Columbus, Ohio 43228.

Published by arrangement with HarperCollins Publishers.
Newfield Publications is a federally registered trademark of
Newfield Publications, Inc.
I Can Read Book is a registered trademark of
HarperCollins Publishers.

DANNY AND THE DINOSAUR
Copyright © 1958 by Syd Hoff
Printed in the United States of America.

All rights in this book are reserved.
No part of this book may be used or reproduced in any
manner whatsoever without written permission except in
the case of brief quotations embodied in critical articles
and reviews. For information address: HarperCollins
Publishers, 10 E. 53rd Street, New York, NY 10022.

Library of Congress Catalog Card Number: 57-7754

Danny and the Dinosaur

One day Danny went

to the museum.

He wanted to see

what was inside.

He saw Indians.

He saw bears.

He saw Eskimos.

He saw guns.

He saw swords.

And he saw . . .

DINOSAURS!

Danny loved dinosaurs.

He wished he had one.

"I'm sorry they are not
real," said Danny.
"It would be nice to
play with a dinosaur."

10

"And I think it would be
nice to play with you,"
said a voice.

"Can you?" said Danny.

"Yes," said the dinosaur.

"Oh, good," said Danny.

"What can we do?"

"I can take you

for a ride,"

said the dinosaur.

He put his head down

so Danny could

get on him.

13

"Let's go!" said Danny.

A policeman stared at them.

He had never seen

a dinosaur stop

for a red light.

The dinosaur was so tall

Danny had to hold up

the ropes for him.

"Look out!" said Danny.

"Bow wow!" said a dog,

running after them.

"He thinks you are a car,"

said Danny. "Go away, dog.

We are not a car."

"I can make a noise

like a car,"

said the dinosaur.

"Honk! Honk! Honk!"

"What big rocks,"
said the dinosaur.

"They are not rocks,"
said Danny.

"They are buildings."

"I love to climb,"

said the dinosaur.

"Down, boy!" said Danny.

21

The dinosaur had to be
very careful not to knock
over houses or stores with
his long tail.

Some people were
waiting for a bus.
They rode on the
dinosaur's tail instead.

"All who want to
cross the street,
may walk on my back,"
said the dinosaur.

"It's very nice of you to
help me with my bundles,"
said a lady.

Danny and the dinosaur

went all over town and

had lots of fun.

"It's good to take an

hour or two off after a

hundred million years,"

said the dinosaur.

They even looked at

the ball game.

"Hit the ball,"

said Danny.

"Hit a home run,"

said the dinosaur.

"I wish we had a boat,"

said Danny.

"Who needs a boat?

I can swim,"

said the dinosaur.

"Toot, toot!"

went the boats.

"Toot, toot!" went Danny

and the dinosaur.

"Oh, what lovely
green grass!" said the
dinosaur. "I haven't
eaten any of that for a
very long time."
"Wait," said Danny. "See
what it says."

PLEASE
KEEP
OFF

They both had ice cream
instead.

"Let's go to the zoo and see
the animals," said Danny.

Everybody came running

to see the dinosaur.

Nobody stayed to see

the lions.

Nobody stayed to see

the elephants.

Nobody stayed to see

the monkeys.

And nobody stayed to
see the seals,
giraffes or hippos,
either.

"Please go away so
the animals will get
looked at,"
said the zoo man.

"Let's find my friends,"

said Danny.

"Very well,"

said the dinosaur.

"There they are,"

said Danny.

"Why, it's Danny riding on

a dinosaur," said a child.

"Maybe he'll give us a ride."

"May we have a ride?"

asked the children.

"I'd be delighted,"

said the dinosaur.

"Hold on tight,"

said Danny.

41

Around and around the
block ran the dinosaur,
faster and faster and faster.

"This is better than a
merry-go-round,"
the children said.

The dinosaur was
out of breath.
"Teach him tricks,"
said the children.

Danny taught the dinosaur

how to shake hands.

"Can you roll over on

your back?"

asked the children.

45

"That's easy,"

said the dinosaur.

"He's smart," said Danny,

patting the dinosaur.

"Let's play hide and seek,"

said the children.

"How do you play it?"

said the dinosaur.

"We hide and you try to

find us," said Danny.

The dinosaur covered

his eyes.

All the children ran

to hide.

The dinosaur

looked and looked

but he couldn't find the children.

"I give up," he said.

Now it was the dinosaur's

turn to hide.

The children covered

their eyes.

The dinosaur hid

behind a house.

The children found him.

He hid behind

a sign.

The children

found him.

He hid behind a

big gas tank.

The children found him.

They found him again

and again and again.

"I guess there's no place

for me to hide,"

cried the dinosaur.

"Let's make believe we

can't find him,"

Danny said.

"Where can he be? Where,

oh, where is that dinosaur?

Where did he go?

We give up,"

said the children.

"Here I am,"

said the dinosaur.

"The dinosaur wins,"

said the children.

"We couldn't find him.

He fooled us."

"Hurrah for the dinosaur!"

the children cried.

"Hurray! Hurray!"

It got late and the other
children left.

Danny and the dinosaur
were alone.

"Well, goodbye, Danny,"
said the dinosaur.

"Can't you come and stay
with me?" said Danny.
"We could have fun."
"No," said the dinosaur, "I've
had a good time—the best I've
had in a hundred million years.
But now I must get back to
the museum. They need
me there."
"Oh," said Danny.
"Well, goodbye."

Danny watched until
the long tail was out
of sight.

Then he went home alone.

"Oh, well," thought Danny,
"we don't have room for a pet
that size, anyway. But we did
have a wonderful day."